CITY OF DOG

CITY OF DOG

GEORGE CHARLTON

BLOODAXE BOOKS

ISBN: 1 85224 266 3

First published 1994 by
Bloodaxe Books Ltd,
P.O. Box 1SN,
Newcastle upon Tyne NE99 1SN.

Bloodaxe Books Ltd acknowledges
the financial assistance of Northern Arts.

Cover printing by J. Thomson Colour Printers Ltd, Glasgow.

Printed in Great Britain by
Cromwell Press Ltd, Broughton Gifford, Melksham, Wiltshire.

For Edmund Smith

There are yet missing of your company
Some few odd lads that you remember not
THE TEMPEST, V.i.

Acknowledgements

Acknowledgements are due to the editors of the following publications in which some of these poems first appeared: *Agenda, Bête Noire, The Echo Room, High on the Walls: A Morden Tower Anthology* (Morden Tower/Bloodaxe Books, 1990), *The Honest Ulsterman, Iron, London Magazine, Poetry Durham, Poetry Review, Poetry with an Edge* (Bloodaxe Books, new edition, 1993), *The Printer's Devil, Sunk Island Review, The Times Literary Supplement*, and *Verse.*

'Seventeen' was broadcast on *Kaleidoscope* (BBC Radio 4).

Contents

CITY

Could man be drunk for ever
With liquor, love or fights,
Lief should I rouse at morning
And lief lie down of nights.

But men at whiles are sober
And think by fits and starts,
And if they think, they fasten
Their hands upon their hearts.

A.E. HOUSMAN

la forme d'une ville-bar
Change plus vite, hélas! que le cœur d'un mortel.

BAUDELAIRE
Le Cygne

Oh would I had never seen Wittenberg, never read book.

MARLOWE,
Dr Faustus, V.ii.

The Drinking Squad's Amnesty

(for J.J. Finch)

We are coming in, past the rented grange,
Its graphic display of yield-economics
Tacked to the wall in the manager's office –

Past the white byre, its ripe fallen dung-fruit.
Tutored in negligence we drifted through harebells,
Their blue haze a dust in a copse by the roadside,

And now we are all coming in. This time on foot
Saving on busfare across from the gates' head,
Goat-leaping a rickety one-span stick bridge.

We have weighed-up the trade shop, the workbench where
The ghost of a skeletal fitter still cleans
A worn out motor with a turps-soaked rag.

But that was the past, before we stepped out
Into the bright aluminium sunlight (which equals
The light on the roof of a warehouse),

Or into the hushed aluminium whispers
Of rain on the roof of a warehouse.
Look out! There is talk of us all coming in,

Armed with a scrupulous anarchy,
To stand among others, just waiting,
All bitchiness and back-biting gone by the board –

To stand, pint in hand, in the midst of a sentence,
With those of no standing at all in their lives,
Fanned by the blowsy plane tree's great boughs.

Melanie's Bar

This bar is a sanctuary
And she, in it, a classic –
Hair down her back,
A fringe on her brow.

She moves from the till
To the handpumps,
To the spirits' bright optics,
And cannot cease to be young.

This is Melanie's –
Whose poised eyes and smile
Are set in the beam
Of a video jukebox.

From pop-socks to pony-tail
Entirely, her scent falls
On this room: drinks,
Left for dead, stand round.

Drinking with My Father's Comrades

(for Sean O'Brien)

They have invited me tonight to drink with them –
These men remote in years from the battle-front
And each one lonely in himself
For that, and for other things.

I take my place among them, eavesdropping
Non-too frequent talk, at their table's
Planetarium in miniature,
Intent, toggle-tongued myself.

They insist all evening they buy me drinks
As one friend 'carrying' another –
An obligation going back to when
Work was never certain, and continued since.

And I permit it, since they do it
For my father's sake: these friends
Who have met in such a way for years,
Whose friendship's something more

Than a limited accomplishment.
This one evening then I will drink with them
Stepping back as it were some thirty
Years and into my father's present:

The chandelier's galaxy of lightbulbs brightens,
And with aplomb a drunk beneath it
Slurs curses at his friend the one-armed bandit,
And night makes mirrors of the lounge-bar windows.

Lovers Meeting in a City Bar

The first kiss, a formal peck,
Is delivered with such pent passion –
As multi-national mergers might progress,
As a bid for mutual concessions.

Round the nape of her neck, shaved clean,
His appley all-compassing biceps reach:
A smirk, a laugh, a crinkled nose – an unpredicted
Richness in the hush of their speech.

Reprobate

He had wafted to my side,
Two yards of stale sweat
Upwind and ripening.
The sepia overcoat, loose-fitting,
Binding his beefy pectorals,
Looked famous, like Balzac's dressing gown.

His finely honed face had a three days' growth
That might have been fashionable
If not merely occasional: beneath it
The cheeks were a mottle – irregular
Blotches on blotches,
An effect much like marble.

And I was thinking: it can't be,
A man who must never wash
From the one same week to the next,
When his take-it-or-leave-it dark eyes
Dilated in polished remembrance
Of discotheque dancefloors, mosaic lights...

Yes, he'd wafted to my side
As if ready for his own bed,
As if our faces mirrored one another
And the glass was heard to say,
'There is always somewhere more,
More, much more incontinent...'

Monsters of the Deep
(for J.J. Wells)

Some singer, poor sod,
Mouth wide open like a bucket,
Is pouring out his heart
Into the Yellow River
But no one takes notice,
Eyes turned instead
Silverly on themselves
In the wall-long bar-room mirror.

They do not notice, even,
Glasses of various
Fill and volume
Raised in effaced hands,
Or the bubble-less lips
Forming shapes for speech.

Nor do they notice
The motion of fingers
Stroking an unseen thigh,
Or these monsters, creeping
Wryly in the mirror,
Flat dilations of themselves.

Still Lucid after All These Beers

(for Spug Ower)

Jostling queues outside a nightclub
Where shoulders, tits, and arses rub
Together with the slap of fists,
With tattooed birds of prey on wrists
Of boy-berserkers, now at ease
From beatings of their winged furies –
Beer-ruddy boys who'll later meet,
Wandering a strict grid of streets,
Calling, and not finding home.
Ah! such is matter for a poem. –
The crowding at the straining doors
Where those still lucid after four
Find out a feel of sun at seven,
The sense of being at one with them
's all wind and piss now...
                    When Tricia,
Seventeen, trainee mortician,
Gargoyle-grim, tear-smudged mascara,
Rebutts her boyfriend's bluff bravura
With, 'Oh so fuckin' faithless sod!
Oh abattoir of would-be love,'
Then up it's thrown – the cry – beer-barbed,
'Me and ye against the warld,'
Or, 'red to white cabbage scatter
Scatter...' as into the gutter
Goes – meat, onion, garnish, pitta –
Slithering a standard doner.
Thus bitter, tart, abrasive speech
Amplifies the trance, the itch;
While permanent, the Dog Star's pall,
Lone, blue, shines on above it all.

The Engulfed Town
(for J.J. Connor)

When wind and tide changed
Engulfing the town,
For good measure it was cased
In aquarium glass,
Where a normal life
Could be resumed
As soon as possible,
Which meant at once.

Now mer-people still
In residence there
Hardly notice grey silt
Piling in doorways,
Or a vague church bell,
If it tolls at all,
Tolls as if tugged
By a submarine undertow.

And each Friday evening,
As is often the case,
Mer-people rub mousse
In their kelp-like hair,
Carefully trim already
Trim beards, or pinch-out
Blackheads at the base of
The nose, before swanning in shoals

To a gig down a hill-street
Where for fathoms lights boogie
In sequence, and where, later,
A much gargled merriment
Comes back along tricking asphalt
Like a burp on the asdic
Of a Home Fleet corvette
Returned from patrol.

Only a quirky amateur
Would dive on it, keen weekend
Marine biologists,
And even they, by now,
Exiled in experience,
Cannot tell why –
Beautiful as children
And dining on rock-strata –

Blanched anemones exhibit
Spores like impetigo,
Or a lustre gone
As on scuffed shoes,
And must persist
In their insistence
Of their total
Ignorance of elsewhere.

Marlborough's Butchers

Offal in tubs might be wigs, doffed
And discarded, as if out of fashion,
By Marlborough's fed-up soldiery.
And smears on white coats could be chocolate,
Or freckles on sleeves beads of paint
From a cot: but of course they are not –
Although the butchers of Marlborough Crescent
Have wives, girlfriends, even children.
They have sex which they joke about
In imaginable ways, as an odd one
Absently scratches his tackle:
There is laughter no end in the loading bay.

Now cold-storage container trucks
Out of Oudenarde and Malplaquet
That brought carcasses wrapped
In muslin like wraiths, have gone:
And the butchers have finished.
They could think they are rid of the weight
Of the beasts from their backs for ever.
But meat slung from hooks might remind them
Of pieces of Europe – such as France, or the split
Halves of Germany newly rejoined,
And a pig's head on a bench, its petrified
Grin, might prompt an imaginable joke,
Such as 'Friend, who's got my arse?'

The Banks of Tyne

Generations of steam locomotives
In passing
Have left the wall-moss black –
Slim ledge upon ledge
Of a sooty reef
Above a ruined pier

Whose waterlogged posts
Take a few testing steps
Into the river
Then seem to hold back.
It is as if they knew
There is now nowhere to go.

On one, a rusted iron ring
Hangs like an eye
With resignation in it.
A skiff may have moored there –
The skiff that would have carried her
Across the water.

Across – and for what? For her
DJ boyfriend's nightly spot
On the discotheque ex-ferry
Tied up down river: dead
In the water, its festive lanterns
Pall in morning light.

Yet the wintry sun's unbelievable
Mediterranean brilliance
Has strength to bring water to the eye.
Across the river, disused staithes
Shine like the skeletal ghost
Of a mammoth unfinished cruiser.

Gateshead, Once Removed

At this distance, and over the river,
These odd few things come to focus:
Blue terraced roofs pitched in waves,
The municipal chamber's high foyer,

And a superstore's promise of largesse;
And the local hotels' back tap-rooms –
Their dank fog of smoke and domino
Boards at which sat our friends,

Those horse and dog lovers,
Who once meant us well. They are all
Still around, and the whistling man,
And the man who would speak with flowers.

Then there's the park and the trees, the scars
Still evident from our Swiss Army knives,
Beside the wide lake and its five-knot ducks
And solitary swan royal-yachting it.

The tips of the branches of a few trees sparkle
In a sunlit patch before rain
Above the cemetery where our relatives
See out the last of themselves.

At this distance, and over the river,
These odd few things come to focus.
A coin, a ticket, would take us there,
But I take it your answer means *No*.

Hippo the Tap-room Oracle

The postman waves at the window cleaner
Waving to him as he wipes the glass
Reflecting Hippo mounting the rungs
Of a ladder propped on a building's lattice.

Hippo is steamy, a sprite among
The monkey-puzzle scaffolding;
Slippery lard in the flooded basements,
Along tuberous, pitch-dark sewers...

Hippo could see from the topmost cornerstone
Of a renovated office block – as far
As the eye could see – regenerated factories
Breathing smokeless air.

Hippo would then rebuild our theatres,
Banks, our shopping precincts, bars –
All lit like the sheen on icing sugar
If it wasn't the fact he knew better.

An Address on the Statues of City Fathers

You elders of the nineteenth-century city,
Industrial magnates, commerce's potentates,

You stand beside roads where old suburbs meet town,
At streets crossing in the centre of the city:

And there you endure – larger than life
And largely ignored, each one of you

Almost in sight of another, and that
Despite the new glassy precincts.

Tactically viewed you are wisely positioned
As though to be urban artillery emplacements.

You Armstrong, and you Whitworth,
Great gun-makers – your breech-loading prototype

Stands in the lobby of a city museum,
Dull and unoiled and a nasty piece of work.

And you Parsons –
Your revolutionary steam-turbines brought us

The dinosaur-dreadnought
Age of Britannia...

Stuck on your sandstone plinths you remain then,
Cocksure and upright as ever you were

And not at all ruffled – not least
By the maimed, the enfranchised pigeons,

Whose freedom it is to sit on your heads.

Beneath the Walls

Beneath pitted sandstone you may walk still,
Alone and tipsy, or linked and in love
A stretch of the wall from a tower's angle
To the place where the city was betrayed
From within: where perhaps a good friend
(He owes you a fiver) a second before
Stepped by the far end: you're not to know
You'll not see him again
More than twelve times in the space of ten years.

Or you may have been one of those lovers
Stood watch in the shadow of the walls,
Cigarette smouldering like a musketeer's match.
If so, then for you, admit that it's tough:
The trace of a scent on your moustache
Recalling that soft brush of lips, that mature
Woman's face (her past different, yet some ways
Similar to your own) restored girlish
Once more in the autumn night's warmth.

Today, it is the spirit of the place
Wrapped in a stained homeless raincoat,
Picks among lettuce leaves three days from fresh,
Soft wrinkled carrot stubs. His dry cider breath
Will curse a bruised apple found on the site
Of the razed priory orchard. Besieged
In himself and bent like a loofah,
Sun striking through an east-facing window
Strikes on him too, facing the day.

Local History

Presently, I will flatten the palm of my hand
Against the brown-ochre stone of the city's
Old town wall. I will wait,
For often they bring up the past here.

For instance, found below Carliol Tower
On the now incomplete circuit of the wall,
A cannonball and a skull –
The one lodged exactly inside the other.

The Sentries' Night-Watch

(West Walls, Newcastle, 1644)

This evening, as we mount the walls,
The housewife, humming a lullaby,
Shakes bedbugs from an eiderdown
Beneath tawny Flemish pantiles:
A lock of loose hair describes her cheek
As thinner than it was in spring.

Atop the castle keep, the flag
That's flown there all along
Is luminous red in the lowering sun:
The captain gives his lass a kiss
Below the steps, his cuirass creaks
In the moistening air of evening coming on.

Our armpits reek: we watch across
The siege-scape's rubbled suburbs,
Its wreckage of coalpits and glasshouses,
The vacant wharfs and merchant-adventurers'
Chambers that rubbery bats rebound off,
To the tree-line of the Scottish wood.

We watch as martins curtly snip through air
To nests like cannonballs beneath the eaves
Of villages we come from – villages
Lost to us, for all the ways are barred,
Though we know their scents of resin and flowers
And their names: Dissington, Dalton, Stamfordham.

Therefore, before we go, we'll leave
Such things we have no further use of –
Our clay-pipe bowls, their broken stems,
The cold scorch of the brazier's fire,
Our long-awaited back-pay in small change:
You can make of them what you like.

City Trails

I

Everlasting beer and rain it proved
All day, but evening turned out fine.
The brewery's tall cooling plant continued
To pump its synthetic by-line,
A cloud-smear shading the parlours,
The kitchens, front and back bedrooms
In districts built for labourers,
While furlongs of varicose tubes
Filled streets invisibly with a ripe stench of hops,
Maddening, appetising, and diverse
As history – and history, I kid not,
Is the thing we were after, of course.

II

Though led, so to speak, by the nose
We couldn't miss signs 'For Sale or Rent' like gibbets
Affixed to unused business premises
Glum now and void as the dark oubliettes
Of a Bluebeard deposed by his people.
Sunbursts changed that, transmuting molten
Window-glass to gold, the supple
Weathercocks set on the cathedral's lantern
To an airy whitened lace.
At a cinema-site under demolition
We were told a dig had found merely the trace
Of coal fires, and coins in small denomination.

III

At last, at West Walls, we'd confront
The towers, basking in their names, dank
Names such as those of recalcitrant
Bullies – Morden, Herber, Stank –
Cross-faces presiding over bin-bags up alleys
Gashed and piled in the manner of corpses.
And there it seemed, immanent, the angry
Missed chances might reveal themselves to us:
A city planner's fabulous design:
Self-governing communities, serene, in league:
Citizens schooled in civics: all combined...
Their innocence, experience, their fatigue.

SEVENTEEN

For Margaret Muse

When and whenever I look at you
Lesbia, the strength of breath goes
    from my voice.
My tongue cleaves to the roof of my mouth,
a thin flame creeps over my limbs,
my ears throb as if inside a bell,
    and my eyes
lose their vision in night.

CATULLUS
translated by Drusty Hare (VI.i. 1967)

Seventeen

'O, Margaret, are you grieving...?'
I'm on the Seventeen and seething
Softly. Again the stomach drops,
Its pangs, like plumb-bobs, will not stop
Until I know it's beaten –
Your parents' strict prohibition
Which makes this, if you've wriggled free,
A lawful criminality

Of sorts. Elsewhere, unquiet might
Be gathered into news: night
Shifts turned back from Motown factories,
The National Guard, laid-back, at ease,
Twirling the baton of Trouble.
Not here – this town fills with couples:
Apprentices are linking lasses,
Ducking heads and stealing kisses.

In stowage bars I'll wait for you,
Scribing a mean hypotenuse
On the wrong side of a beer mat.
The theorem I'll construct will prove
Pythagoras is down the tubes;
A circle squared will demonstrate
At this stage, all is possible...
Our first explorative night at it:

Two grey irises like snowflakes,
The feverish limbs, the tiny quakes
Along the spine – my touch of flu.
Did you then know all this, when you,
With well-intentioned lover's hands
Put me to bed like contraband,
And in the dark returned a grin,
And with those hands, then, tucked me in?

White Hot Technology

A warm puff like wind
Is not enough
Though you pump and pump
With a wild happy passion
The gasfire's pilot-light:
A flame, anaemic,
Tipped rowanberry-bright,
Flares – flares and falters.
'Try saying that
With sinuses blocked,' you call,
A bruise-fingered girl
Stretched on the fender-mat,
Leaving the light to rest
For a while. While outside,
Framed in the fire-breast
Mirror, beyond the raw window,
A man in an ex-army
Greatcoat bobs by –
Face like a teacake,
Goodwill in a pint pot,
A blurred woolly dollop
Like what on his head.
He is here to sweep leaves –
Those you saw scattered
Like citizens from gunshot:
They've surrendered in heaps
To him, laying down arms by the grey
Churchyard wall. He peeps
In on us again, immune,
His numb face number
Than numb. 'That one,' you say,
'Was once a gas plumber.'

The Supremes' *Greatest Hits*

The nightclub is moon-colour,
A blackboard's chalky darkness
Where moonlight spills over
Crisp walls, across the floor,
Ourselves dancing on it. 'Like us,'
I say, 'it has made it so far

By cancelling all past warranty,
All that which is not vital...'
I would reach for a daisy
Stencilled in moon-glow,
Stroke at each odd petal
Daring only to say 'You love me,'

And, 'The moon is your buoyant face,
Its lunar corona your hair,
Apt emblem of this,
Diana's latest song –'
But my thumb, like a reed, is here
At my mouth, wetted on lip and tongue.

Snapshot from a Daytrip

There you are, middle-distant
On the shoreline,
Some of those thousands
Of millions of sand-grains
Sluicing between your bare toes.

The yellow of your T-shirt
Is such
It waves and shouts almost,
Unfocussing the clarity
Of your fine-boned face.

Out of frame – I knew then,
And remember now –
Is the mass of the Bass Rock,
Its inert and dark cloud
Weighting our horizon.

Backlanes

There are still backlanes some couples use,
Their secondhand cars sprouting all over
A misty film composed
Of thousands of tiny beads
Of moisture:
Lit by streetlamps they glisten;
And what you take at first to be head-rests,
Are two heads, kissing.

Twocked

Police slang: 'Taken without owner's consent'

It is the morning after the morning
After a Friday night out.

On land that lies waste –
That was once a school field –

There stands the squat wreck
Of a 'C' reg. Metro City,

Its flame-tinctured body-work
Still tingling with heat.

From heat-fractured tubing
A sigh, a brief sigh,

Is sadder than the saxophones
Of Holland–Dozier–Holland.

The radio-cassette
Has been taken from its slot:

An unlooted tape
Has congealed in smoked plastic:

A dangling talisman no longer tells
Memento Mori or *Carpe Diem.*

While the clicking of the metal as it cools
Is like a telephone about to ring,

A voice, anticipated, about to break
The news – the composed voice

In no way like
The voice transfixed in this burnt-out wreck.

Picking up Love's Meal Bill

I love you when you leave,
Though when you leave
My stomach rides a North Sea
Swell, and the lungs heave.

I love the way you eat
Fettucini – its tiny spots
Of sauce sprayed star-wise
Across the table cloth.

And I love the way your lips,
Withdrawing from a cup,
Leave dribble, and the way
The blistered thumb turns up.

I love the way those lips
And fingertips caress
The table napkin, dabbing,
Dabbing at the mess.

I love you for the timing
Of your laugh –
Abrupt, always welcome,
Catching, like a cough.

And I love you for the fact
That when we've parted,
We've parted lovers as always –
Going Dutch, big-hearted.

Tanka

I

Roads are unravelling
Their red and yellow yarn.
It peels from the sweater you wear
Revealing, each moment,
More of your midriff.

II

I'm choked: is it
The hundreds of thousands
Of kisses you gave me,
Or a bracelet of hair
In my throat?

III

On the Berwick Road
In the Kyloe Hills
A small bird with a big voice
– Whose name I couldn't name –
Called your name.

IV

Clouds cruise south,
And never the same cloud twice.
Those distant must be over your house.
Look! See – that's me!
I'm the cloud in pants.

V

Wind in the phone wires
Is the sound of your voice.
The poles make huge steps
In your direction: I follow
At a tight-rope walker's pace.

VI

I have your scarf at my throat,
A bangle of cold
On the wrist of each gloved hand.
Glancing at my face in a shopfront
I am old without you.

VII

Water flowing through tree-tops
Is the wind in these silent parts.
In my mind's wide-open eye
I make your hair blond wheat,
Your throat a rippling stream.

VIII

Silence and the wind,
Cloud-caps on Cheviot,
And a sudden blink of washing
Fluttering brief semaphore:
Message received and understood.

IX

And all at once you're with me,
Amidst acres of wheat shoots,
Skeletons of trees in bud,
In a land made different, made green,
By a different light.

The Girlhood of Iseult

Clearly, I can see your past:
The isolated lodge
On the old road to the coast;
The girls, all sisters, younger
Than yourself – white knees, white
Ankle socks startle the grass.

There is an old horse, bridled,
And about to be saddled,
A dismantled motorbike
In the shade of the wall:
And the girls are at play
With maimed dolls, or matches.

I can see you stand apart,
Raised hand at your brow –
A salute to the strength of light.
You are wearing a light-checked girl's
Summer frock, pre-puberty's last,
As you turn your gaze to the fields,

To the shipyard cranes as far
As the sea, charting the course
Of the river. At the drop
Of a match the first crop's
Stooks will suddenly catch, the air
Smear with a watery glaze.

Costa del Luna

We have taken this room
From our youth, and now
At a pre-arranged signal —
The twilit hotel shedding
Its heat, the overhead fan
Shut down for the night —

Again, cast-off for the blue.
Clocks might as well stop, dim plants
Wrap it up, save for their leaves'
Paced breathing. We cool, too,
In the skin's alabaster,
Our sweat a crystalline balm.

The moon is a radiant disc,
A porthole wide open all night,
Through which we can hear a dog-bark,
The rasp of an anchor chain
Clanking... Now, drifting in view
Is a cloud-archipelago.

We lie here improving ourselves
By the minute — mute limpets
Eased from obligatory rocks:
'You must see no bad in me,'
You say, at last, getting away
With a liberty this time.

Beadnell

It's as if we have lived here
A lifetime, and in that time
Name-tagged and photographed
(Full-face and profile, both)
Each grain of sand, while the sea
Reflexively cleared its throat

In the distance, and the sand
Between high and low water
Was an ever-wet gloss. The sea
Frets now, seabirds hurl abuse,
And our hats, doffed by the wind,
Take the waves' deep applause.

Ours are minds at a tilt,
Like the globe on its axis,
Where the flash of a gull's white
Wing span, against an impasto
Of grey-purple cloud, is
The smile on a rained-on face.

It is here the last pay load
Is the size of a coble,
Its fantail butted by surf,
And sand-dells are ruined
Sub-Siberian townships
Known only to stamp dealers.

While the walls of the lime kilns
Are a gun-fort's ramparts
Circa the heyday of piracy,
And we, its only/last
Caretaker-governors, captains
Of rain squall and sunburst.

Borderline

At the very edge of summer,
And with autumn just over
The next field boundary,
In a hall at the end of
An unmetalled drive, he waits
For her, hapless ephebe.

It might exist for them only –
This darkling window-view,
This hall and its firs, screening
The road she'll return on;
This mist, gathered like kapok
Out of a day without context.

On the terrace a hare crops
Clover... And he glimpses
The visitors' book, its list
Of infinite aliases,
And detention is brought to mind,
And the Latin verb 'Amo'.

Then he turns to the window
And under his breath might say:
'Yes, take all my clothes now
And I'll go naked for you,'
As she pulls to the door, with night,
And cancels all difference.

Cabin Fever

He is mate on the outbound
SS Belle Dame Sans Merci
At watch by the binnacle,
Reefer buttoned to his neck.
The bridge rail is icy
Beneath a perfect half moon,
Its ever-fresh lemon slice
About to drop from the sky.

Waves weave a sea-duvet, teeth
Chatter in his head. As he scans
The paling lexicon of stars
Phosphor winks at the prospect
Of a pink-gin sunrise.
And a voice, the sweet siren
Voice of a saltwater craving
Intones from the rigging:

He might tread, in the wake
Of a Henry or Vasco,
A disenchanted chart –
No one-eyed, green-eyed monster,
No planters on the whale's back,
Only the stolid set-square
And fine dividers laid aside:
And his mind, off on a tangent.

The Girl Next Door

There was a railing with rust,
A laurel bush, forsythia,
Roses, convolvulus, and
A dwarf hydrangea between us.

And an older brother,
Seventeen years a consort
Of sorts. Most of the time
They got on well together.

His friends were hers: she went out
With a tall one in leathers,
And another the double
Of Hotspur – cuddly, stout.

She'd walk to school with no socks,
And sometimes I'd walk beside
Her. Once we shared an apple
And a choc-bar from her lunch box.

It was her hair I'd noticed,
Fair, curled along the curve
Of an ear – her eyes, her eye-lids:
I thought I was an artist.

And once, wearing a dress,
Black, like a silhouette, she danced
With me, and I (it was an
Accident) softly brushed her breast.

Whole days I didn't see
Her – the absence of her voice
Across the fence, the street
Vacant as a blank TV.

But there were the nights. Every
Night our beds lay side by side –
The bed-springs, through the wall
Between us, gasping loudly.

Mini

Purgatorial Mini
Of youth, your heart's turned aside
And the radiator grill
Allows any filth in.
On wet roads you are drowned
When brash juggernauts pass.

Dashboard of the simpleness
Of an early Sopwith Pup –
O, and Radio Caroline,
And the feel of an Airfix kit.
I was co-pilot
In your $1/72$ scale cockpit.

You could turn on a sixpence,
Take us miles on five gallons,
But at lights allowed others
To look down on us – not
That we gave a shit then.
We would have died in you,

Squashed flat, our entrails entwined.
You cramped love on the backseat,
As if designed by a prude
To put off the young –
But in you we persisted,
Revving, trembling, stalling.

DOG

Rain is the sound of stiff polythene sheets
Spread by a mindful furniture porter,
But the bursting bladders of stinging cold
Have caught out angels in a cemetery close by.
It is the kiss of death for the foggy suburbs...
Indoors, also, has its regular performance:
The finicky cat at her aerobic ablutions,
The falsetto gasfire throwing its voice, and the clock
About to come down with bronchitis.
While from a dog-eared, dog-smelling, pack of cards –
A bequest of the previous tenant –
The Queen of Spades and street-wise Knave of Hearts
Tête à tête whisper of trumped affairs.

> BAUDELAIRE
> Les Fleurs du mal, LXXV

Benton Static

Whatever it has to mean, it has to do
With the fact that the generator
Has its own life to live, humming
Its own tune, mirthful, atonal;
With the tall whitethorn hedges
Thickening in season
As they have done for centuries.

It has something to do with a hidden paddock
Orphaned at the end of an unadopted lane,
New grass growing back at the edges,
The clover-munching sheep grazing there;
And an amateur gardener standing at ease
Resting the tip of his hoe
On a green raft adrift in leafy suburbs.

Somehow my own house is involved in it,
Its useless chimney stacks reduced,
The curtains drawn in the children's room
Already. And my neighbour:
His skill as a tradesman, the sizeable
Mortgage, like me, he inherits; his own business
Run from the back of a secondhand van.

Above all it has something to do
With this enduring northern twilight,
A blackbird's uninterrupted song
In the midst of deep shrubbery.
It is two men on a pavement,
Strangers in passing, acknowledging
One another's solitary presence.

Descartes at No.1

A couple, arm in arm, of middle years
But young, young looking,
Stroll slowly in the street's
First long spring evening.
They glance at a sale board,
Glance up at windows – a dark shine
That gives nothing away.

If they want, they can imagine
The gas ring's blue smile,
The fan-assisted oven's
Arcane balmy bluster – and Descartes
Pottering in the kitchen.
He, too, once had the knack,
A stranger's familiarity,

A way of nodding at crocuses,
Of showing feeling for snowdrops
Much raided by birds.
Head inclined to one side
In the natural light, he wondered then
How it might be
He could live on this street, live here.

Where We Used to Live

People, if they lived in rings
    could walk in curves:
their natural streets would then be arcs,
    off-cuts of a wide
yet still unfinished circle.
    But there we lived, *mutatis mutandis*,
in a linear community
    where our neighbours were known to us
mostly by voices – and then usually
    suddenly raised and dramatic,
as in Shakespeare's problem-family plays.
    At weekends they were known to us
only by sight: for instance,
    caught from a window
overlooking a garden
    in which doubtless lay buried
a tall Saxon thegn, where proprieties
    of dress had long gone by the board
and they dressed in *The Sweater*
    Of The Rotted Oxter.

However, they were not known to us
    by sight and voice together.
Although – what with paper lamp-globes
    aglow in their living-rooms,
bright as grain for the famished places:
    what with the way they sat
at the television, their silhouettes
    in highlight like some several
Ladies (and Gentlemen) of Shalott:
    and what with music centres,
their electric saws, and astonishingly
    even the click of wooden pieces
on their chessboards –
    it could hardly be said of them
they kept themselves to themselves.

On a Station of the Metro

A bashed-about silver reflector,
Sprayed slogans and a few proper names –
One my own though I'm not guilty –
Affront the pensioned-off,
The 10 a.m. loose-enders
Standing round.

Behind us, groin-buffed turnstiles,
The membrane-treated roofs
Of grant-improved
Turn of century terraced dwellings,
And a fuzz of tall weeds – acres
Where sidings were dismantled.

And further, a new factory unit,
Its burnished wastepipes
Steaming in the sun,
Seems to signify light industry
Might ease the terse
Impoverishment of place.

A late garden bloom,
Taken root between sleepers,
Is as wan as the faces of those waiting,
One of whom remarks
He could pluck it for his buttonhole,
Or to place behind an ear.

Greensleeves in the Fifties

Where notes on the sheet stop
She stops – a seven year old
Strawberry blonde laying
Aside her first recorder,
And *Greensleeves*'s consigned to the past.

She'll have nothing more to do
With it, its chords dark as pockets,
And would walk straight from the room
But cannot find the door: worse,
The air stays in her head.

Shut in another shaded room
Topsy gives out a suffocated whinge:
The clock tocks to itself,
Listlessly, or to the heavy
Black oak table laid for tea.

There, a slab of butter, bared,
Has chiselled into it, and gracelessly,
The footprints of a fly, as if it were
Snow melting in a garden
Or sand frozen by the shoreline.

On the taciturn piano
Ants colonise a galaxy of apples
Rimming the sable bowl,
As a defunct gas bracket
Queries the wall it depends from –

While shimmering, unblinking,
A lightbulb looks for company
And finds it, on a chair,
In a copy of *The Beano*,
The girl's bum-print on it.

i.m. Lesley Waters

My roundabout routes
Homeward from school
Were designed with her
In mind: the trail

Across terraced districts,
The acute ascent of steps
Where it hurt to peek
Too far into her dress.

I scarcely knew Lesley Waters
Then, and what I felt
Was hardly clear to myself.
So really it couldn't matter

When later I heard
Of the first husband, or
Met her steering a pushchair
Through a tinny arcade.

What she made of her life
Was a moderate mess,
Much as the most of us,
And is as nothing now

But the girl I dared never
Ask out – hand on rail,
One leg raised, and ever
A few steps ahead.

La Mer

The voice of the singer of *La Mer*
Came on over the waves from a French
Radio station. For a long stretch the sand
Ran down to the sea, and the sea itself
Was a dazzling field of chrome:
It and the sky had potential
Like walls in a flat freshly painted.
A young man wearing a shirt
The tincture of sand chewed
On a Gauloise and mimed the song,
Rocking the girl in his cradled arms
Quietly. A beer can cooling in the shade
Of a rock was an emblem of one
Of many cans that season
Trodden in the sand. A smart
Sea-breeze brought tears to the eyes
Of the young man and the girl
In a moment that for them
Both could and could not last.
For you then E.S. and you R.R.
Friendship tipped out like sand from a shoe:
The dial on the radio slipped
From the station, the wavebands crackled
Like a beer can crushed.

Come Back Peter Pan

Darling has
A missing stud
Mrs Darling's pippins bud
– *Come back Peter Pan*

Wendy, dear
Bed's not the same
Your sheets are stained, you have a pain?
– *Come back Peter Pan*

Michael, John
Pity you ran
The Audit had a rescue plan
– *Come back Peter Pan*

Nana, kids
Were not enough
Without them life is rough *ruff ruff*
– *Come back Peter Pan*

Tinker Bell
Your fairy dust
Became a Boeing bomber's ghost
– *Come* in *Peter Pan*

The Lost Boys
Have been booked at last
For drunkenness and breaking glass
– *Come back Peter Pan*

Captain Hook
They have your files
The wards are full of crocodiles
– *Come back Peter Pan*

Mr Smee
We need a favour:
Foam the soap and strop that razor
– *Come back Peter Pan*

Pirates, brave lads,
Your ships were scrapped
At Dunston and at Jarrow Slack
– *Come back Peter Pan*

Tiger Lily
The bath is filling
The knots they bound you with are swelling
– *Come back Peter Pan*

The alarm clock's
Digits blink
And blink: it dreams, perhaps it thinks?
– *Come back Peter Pan*

Peter, pal,
You'll not survive
A musical revival
– Piss off while you can

Peter and Wendy

Peter and Wendy both have the same place of work,
Which makes things handy: on workday
Mornings they take it in turn
To drive each other there. Promotion
Doesn't come quickly in the Administration
Section, but it comes.

Lately they have moved into their third
Home together. The first, when they married,
Was a rented flat: now
They have a house with two spare bedrooms –
One set aside for Peter's friend Jas
Should he stay at weekends.

Friday is Peter's night out with the boys.
Wendy meets her girlfriends,
And both meet with each other
For one last drink at the end of the evening.
On Saturdays, sometimes, they go to the cinema,
But less often now than they used to.

Recently, Peter bought a CD unit...
Waiting with Wendy for the late-night bus
He thinks of this, his old mono Hi-Fi,
And of the first two LPs he ever owned:
Bob Dylan's fifth – *Bringing It All Back Home* –
And The Beatles' *Help*.

In the Cul de Sac of Ménage à Trois

Your house – it's sad, this kitchen dim,
Spirits that inhabit here
Indifferent, or else outdoors,
And the atmos – *ugh!* – the atmosphere

Is something else: an odour
Of damp clothes, the washing-machine
Defending its corner, inert,
Resentful of a sudsy routine.

At least, seemingly, you please
The fridge, offering propitiously
A bottle, a milky appeasement,
Accepted apparently.

Yet its flex, a tendrilled ivy,
Is tightening its grip, machismo
As your husband – your husband
Of whom you have said: 'Like so

Much make-believe he cannot
Be believed.' As he has said, often:
'It's difficult not to think of a wife
And at the same time another woman.'

And this while your young son slept on
In his dream of bad monsters.
And to think, at a takeaway, once,
Two drunks mistook us for lovers.

The Widows at the Club

It is all they've inherited from late husbands –
Life membership to the workingmen's club
And woe-betide the stranger mistakenly taking
One of the chairs from the table they sit at
Habitually each week, the only night out
Allowed them by pensions which are otherwise
So eaten into by things.

Their lipsticked cupid bows are askew
On slackened muscles and lines round their mouths:
Mingled raw scents of perfumes taint
The taste of cherry brandies and substitute champagnes.
And always it is they who seem just to have missed
That one last number on the bingo card: when one
Or another collects a round from the bar
The jackpot 'that jackpot' is as far-off as ever.

At the end of the evening's entertainment they will sing,
They will take a little longer than is usual
To check in their handbags for the keys to the flat,
To find a cardigan or a glove. And outside
Where one or two avenues of streetlamps come together
They will take a little longer than most others
To make their goodbyes, to say 'Goodnight'...
The flats where they live are so awkwardly built
Their coffins will end as their husbands' coffins
Stuck fast in tight passageways.

Flodden Field

A veneer of Flodden dew
And pollen distils
On your boots, and you look
To the two smooth hills,

The few dozen acres
Of wheat, hedge-quartered,
To the combine taking
The incline steadily.

Here history has made
The landscape significant,
Made daisies heraldic
On a field vert.

As likely as not your Scottish
And my English ancestors
Confronted one another
Across this field that day,

As even now our children
Squabbling at the foot
Of the memorial's plinth
Will not heed warning.

Try telling them of Flodden:
The close assault of arms –
The pike, the bill, the sword –
Will be scissors, paper, stone.

The *SS City of Dog*

She has wintered in the Baltic –
Morning and evening twilight
The same, the long grey bit
In between, the same:
A white light at the mast-head,
Green and red on either beam.

Last of a merchant line
Her red duster cracks at the stern;
Her heading, the harbour bar,
Where black-back philosopher
Gulls shear wildly away
At the approach of the pilot boat.

She has coasted the coastline
Beneath the blurred faces
Of gouache-washed clouds, a breath
Of inland wild garlic
On the off-shore breeze,
And stoppered Armada guns

Breasting a battery; past the shag
And the guillemot
Who, poised on rock islands,
Live on their nerves' edge;
Past tank-traps, concrete pill-boxes
Idling in sand, the odd

Embattled barbed-wire
Emplacement, and couples
Linked on the beaches
Wide open to privacy.
The land's well-kept secret
Hurts no one (who does not know).

Here, at the harbour mouth,
Spring's first weekend trippers
Wave from an outward-bound ferry
(Newcastle-Amsterdam-Bruges)
Impatient for duty-frees,
For each other – or both.

And paid-off, in hock, her seamen
Return to doors of scabbed paint –
Those odd and even numbers –
To red coals in grates piled high,
High as Bali Ha'i, burning
To welcome them home.

And the mate, imagine him,
A latter-day Tristan,
Calling, ship-to-shore,
Regardless of listeners
Listening in – 'Drusty here:
Is that Iseult?'

The *SS Lady Iseult*

She is laid up on one of
The many rivers in Armorica,
Her reckless beauty subdued
For a while. Miles from the sea
The skin of her hull
Exudes the sea's seasoning.

She catches a whiff of the sea
When electric trains pass
At the end of the creek.
Reflections of lamps on the water
Make for a miniature
Midsummer aurora.

And even the steward, of her
Skeleton crew, chain-smoking
At the rail between sittings,
Can't miss the hawthorn's white
Scented blizzard, the lilac bulbs
Dripping from the bank above.

Home at last, and not at home,
A cuckoo among a flock
Of different birds, she does not look
To the long-term. The women
Of this place converse gently:
Their men have strolled to the pub.

At twilight the face of the moon
Shows ring-worm; faint ripples
Sucking the waterline
Are kisses of neat toxic nymphs,
Creakings in the teak-work
Their whispering voices

Berthed between decks. While the mate,
Resembling an ageing scholar
Recalls a well-thumbed almanac,
Frail thesaurus of tenderness,
In which he might look for a tide-change,
The difference of lust and love.